D1716606

Fact Finders®

Landmarks in U.S. History

THE GROUNDBREAKING
PONY EXPRESS

by Patricia R. Quiri

CAPSTONE PRESS
a capstone imprint

Fact Finder Books are published by Capstone Press,
1710 Roe Crest Drive, North Mankato, Minnesota 56003
www.mycapstone.com

Library of Congress Cataloging-in-Publication Data
Names: Quiri, Patricia Ryon, author.
Title: The groundbreaking Pony express / by Patricia R. Quiri.
Description: North Mankato, Minnesota : Capstone Press, [2017] | Series: Fact
    finders. Landmarks in U.S. history. | Includes index.
Identifiers: LCCN 2017003797 (print) | LCCN 2017020597 (ebook) |
    ISBN 9781515771425 (eBook PDF) | ISBN 9781515771159 (library hardcover) |
    ISBN 9781515771388 (pbk.)
Subjects: LCSH: Pony express—History—Juvenile literature. | Postal
    service—United States—History—Juvenile literature.
Classification: LCC HE6375.P65 (ebook) | LCC HE6375.P65 Q57 2017 (print) |
    DDC 383/.1430973—dc23
LC record available at https://lccn.loc.gov/2017003797

Editorial Credits
Bradley Cole and Gena Chester, editors; Sarah Bennett and Brent Slingsby, designers;
Pam Mitsakos, media researcher; Steve Walker, production specialist

Photo Credits
Alamy: ClassicStock, 8 bottom left, Nat Holt Productions/AF archive, 29; Bridgeman Images: © Look and
Learn, 17, J.T. Vintage, 10; Getty Images: Bettmann, cover, Corbis, 15, Ed Vebell, 19; Newscom: akg-images,
9, Everett Collection 25, UPPA/Photoshot, 1; North Wind Picture Archives: 6–7, 20–21, 24, 27 top right, 28;
Wells Fargo Historical Services: Photo used with Permission from Wells Fargo Bank, N.A., 22; Shutterstock:
cristi180884, 27 top left, Justin Mair, 4–5, nicemonkey, 16 bottom left, Topuria Design, 16 bottom middle,
vectorkat, 16 bottom right; SuperStock: 23; Wikimedia: Nara, 11; XNR Productions:
XNR/Map, 13

Design Elements:
Shutterstock: Andrey_Kuzmin, ilolab, Jacob J. Rodriguez-Call, Jessie Eldora Robertson, Olga Rutko

Printed and bound in the USA
010399F17

TABLE OF CONTENTS

EXPRESS ROUTE

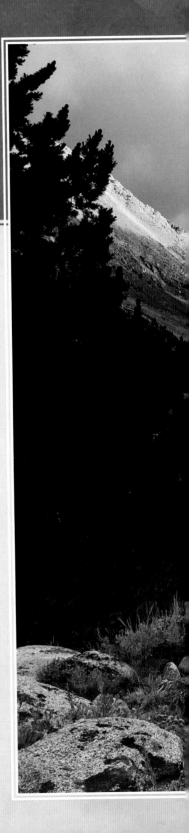

A lone rider raced through the rough mountain path. He was only 16 years old and looked small atop his powerful horse. He leaned lower over its mane and picked up speed. As a Pony Express rider, his job was to be fast. He and the other riders had a limited amount of time to get mail to Sacramento, California. Not a second could be wasted on the long, cross-country route.

He was only a couple of miles out from the next Pony Express station. Another rider in the relay would be waiting to take the letters the rest of the way — or so he hoped. He had heard rumors of Paiutes, a local American Indian tribe, attacking stations. He pushed his horse faster. Out on the frontier anything was possible, and everything was dangerous.

an empty trail in the Rocky Mountains

The Pony Express used a relay system. Each rider covered certain sections of the almost 2,000-mile (3,219-kilometer) route. At the end of one section, another rider would be waiting to carry the mail. The relay of horses, riders, and rest stations went from Missouri to California.

Getting west was not easy. Riders traveled over mountains and through deserts. American Indians controlled much of the western territory. And some tribes were unhappy with white settlers entering their land. But not even the summer heat, winter snow, and hostile tribes could stop the Pony Express riders.

A Pony Express rider arriving at a rest station.

How It Began

More than 100,000 people had moved to California during the 1849 Gold Rush. Their numbers continued to grow. At the time the **telegraph** was the fastest way to communicate. But telegraph wires did not yet reach all the way across the country. It was important to people and government officials living in the West to keep in touch with those in the East. Many were anxious for news about the looming Civil War (1861–1865). The demand for fast communication sparked the creation of the Pony Express, which began in 1860.

"The mail must go through" was the Pony Express motto. And it did. For the one and a half years of its existence, the Pony Express was the fastest mail-delivery service to California. The U.S. government benefited from the Pony Express's fast service. They were thrilled to receive mail and news in the promised 10 days. The public greatly admired the **dedication** of the Pony Express riders. But the Pony Express didn't get started quickly. It took time, money, and planning.

telegraph—a machine that uses electronic signals to send messages over long distances

dedication—devotion; the act of giving your time, effort, or attention to some purpose

JOURNEYING WEST

Many settlers heading to California during the 1849 Gold Rush passed through Missouri. The well-stocked towns along the banks of the Missouri River provided supplies the settlers needed for the trip. The Midwest became a natural **gateway** to California.

DID YOU KNOW?

Before the Pony Express, some mail was shipped to what is today Panama in Central America. From there it was carried across Panama to the Pacific Ocean. The mail was then put on another ship bound for California.

Independence, Missouri, around 1855

One concern for new settlers of the West was mail service — it was slow and **infrequent**. Mail sent by boat could take several months. Once mail finally arrived at the California coast, much of it still had to travel to those living inland. One man delivered mail from the main post offices to the mining camps. He charged 1 ounce (28 grams) of gold dust per letter and 2 ounces (56 g) for newspapers.

Eventually, the government began sending mail overland instead of by sea. Overland mail could follow two trails — a southern route or a northern-central route. The northern way was shorter. But because of rough trail conditions, only one rider at a time could travel through it during the winter months.

....

gateway—a place where people can enter a region
infrequent—not happening very often

In the late 1850s, slavery was a huge **political** issue. It even affected mail delivery. The U.S. **postmaster general**, a southerner, preferred mail to be carried along the southern route. While the southern route was safer, the postmaster general also had political reasons for his preference. He hoped this service would encourage settlers to move into slave states and territories. That way, slavery might be expanded into the southwestern territories.

In the 1900s, the Pony Express was sometimes called the Pony Post.

But the **freighting** company of Russell, Majors, and Waddell had other plans. The owners were determined to get a contract from the U.S. government to carry mail along a northern-central route. William Russell had an idea that he hoped would "build a worldwide reputation" for his company. Russell suggested a relay system between men on horseback. Riders would travel light — carrying only mail, newspapers, and telegrams. Stations would provide fresh horses and riders along the way.

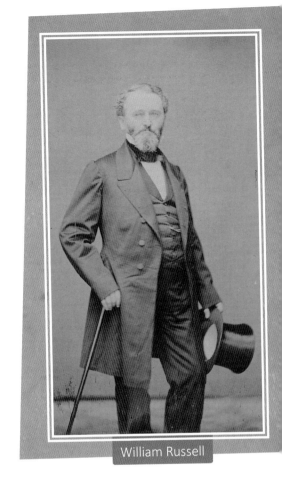
William Russell

Russell hoped a "pony express" would prove that the northern route was the way to transport mail. He also hoped that his company would be well paid by the government to deliver mail to the West. Late in 1859, Russell, Majors, and Waddell formed the Central Overland California & Pikes Peak Express Company. Through that, the Pony Express was created.

political—of or relating to the government

postmaster general—the head of the government's postal, or mail delivery, system

freighting—transporting large amounts of goods

PREPARATIONS

The Central Overland Company had much to do to organize the Pony Express. Horses and ponies had to be bought. Riders and station workers had to be hired, and some new stations needed to be built. The plan called for each rider to carry mail for about 75 miles (121 km). Riders would stop every 10 or 15 miles (16 or 24 km) at a relay station to switch horses. At the 75-mile (121-km) mark, another rider would be ready with a fresh horse to begin the next long run.

On March 31, 1860, the St. Joseph Weekly West newspaper proudly announced that St. Joseph, Missouri, would be the eastern end of the Pony Express. The Pony Express had about 160 stations. The route went from St. Joseph to Sacramento. This was a distance of nearly 2,000 miles (3,218 km). Some stations already existed, and many more were quickly built.

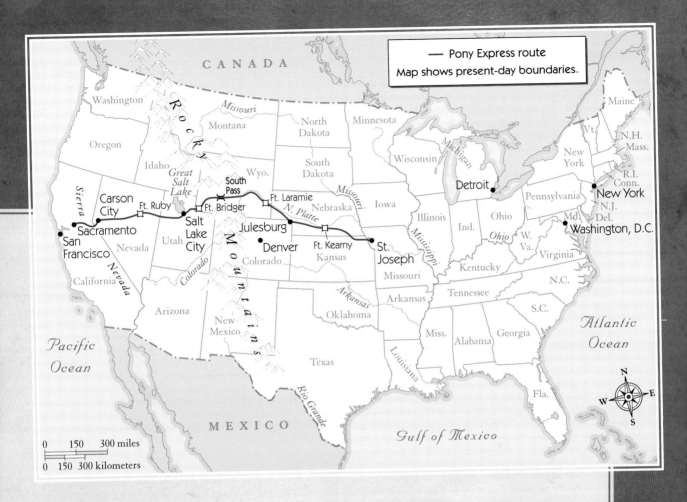

The route roughly followed the Mormon and Oregon-California trails. It included modern-day Kansas, Nebraska, Colorado, Wyoming, Utah, Nevada, and California.

The company bought about 400 horses. Some of them were wild mustangs found in western United States. These horses were used to the hot desert climate. Others were Kentucky thoroughbreds, bred for speed. Horses had to be able to run 12 or 13 miles (19 or 20 km) without stopping.

Riders earned $50 to $100 a month, which was a good wage in those days. Working for the Pony Express could be dangerous, though. Riders delivered mail no matter what the weather — rain, hail, or snow. The trail consisted of rough **terrain** and there was little help for riders in danger. This was especially true in the far West. The route cut right through the Paiute Indian territory. Paiute Indians were angry with the increasing number of travelers going through their homeland. Because of this, riders and stations in the West risked attack.

But plenty of young men still wanted to ride for the Pony Express. About 80 riders were needed to keep the Pony Express in motion. Many of those hired were still teenagers. The Central Overland Company was very strict about the behavior of its employees. Each person had to sign an **oath** declaring that he would not use bad language or drink alcohol.

Each station had workers who took care of the horses. If the station was also used for **stagecoaches** or other travelers, it had several employees and more animals. Many stations, especially in the desert, were lonely and rugged. Often they were no more than a shack or even a large hole dug out of a hillside.

terrain—the surface of the land
oath—a serious, formal promise
stagecoach—a horse-drawn vehicle for carrying people and goods

an off-duty pony express rider

15

Riders used mochilas, important equipment specially made for the Pony Express. This leather cover fit over the horse's saddle. Each rider needed two mochilas. One was to carry mail from east to west and another to carry mail from west to east. Each mochila had four boxlike pockets that held the mail. The rider kept the mochila in place with his legs as he rode. When it was time for a fresh horse, the mochila could easily be slipped off the tired horse and onto the next one.

Mail would cost $5 per half ounce, which was very expensive then. But the mail would arrive in California from St. Joseph in just 10 days! Something that was unheard of at the time.

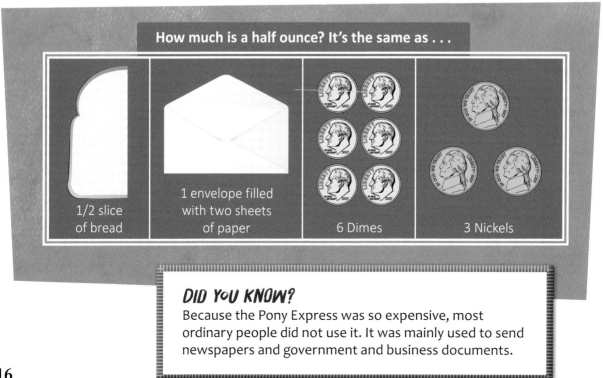

How much is a half ounce? It's the same as . . .

| 1/2 slice of bread | 1 envelope filled with two sheets of paper | 6 Dimes | 3 Nickels |

DID YOU KNOW?
Because the Pony Express was so expensive, most ordinary people did not use it. It was mainly used to send newspapers and government and business documents.

Pony Express riders did not wear uniforms. Instead, they wore what was appropriate for the weather on their route. They usually dressed in buckskin shirts, regular trousers, boots, and a hat. The only guns they carried for protection were revolvers. Rifles were considered too heavy and might slow down the horses.

THE PONY EXPRESS IS OFF!

4

Because the Pony Express charged so much money to deliver a letter, its operators promised the fastest delivery possible. Riders had strict schedules to keep, no matter what the weather or situation.

On April 3, 1860, a crowd gathered in St. Joseph to see a young man take off on the first Pony Express run. The first rider is believed to have been either Johnny Fry or Billy Richardson. Whoever he was, he could not leave until he had the mail. A messenger was supposed to bring mail gathered in Washington, D.C., New York, and Detroit, Michigan. But he missed a train connection from Detroit to Missouri and was two hours late.

The crowd cheered when they finally heard a whistle announce the arrival of the train. Company officials took the letters from the messenger and packed them in the mochila. At 7:15 p.m. the rider swung the mochila onto the horse. He sped off as the crowd cheered and a cannon blasted.

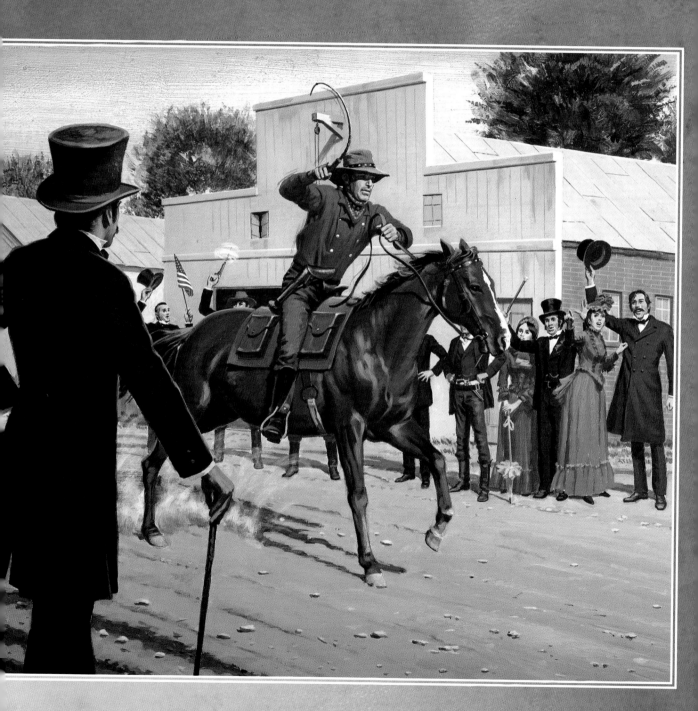

Across the country in California, the people of San Francisco enjoyed their own celebration. The first eastbound Pony Express rider boarded a boat with another mochila filled with mail. He handed off the mail to the next rider at Sacramento. The rider then began his journey east and later passed on the mochila to Warren Upson at Sportsman's Hall, a Pony Express station.

Upson spent most of his first ride trying to make a trail through the deep snow of the Sierra Nevada mountains. But he finished his challenging run on time. Celebrations rang out again in Missouri and California when the mail was delivered. Newspapers praised the achievement and printed stories that arrived by Pony Express.

Riders often faced rough weather on their runs.

5

DANGEROUS RIDES

Robert "Pony Bob" Haslam rode one of the most dangerous sections of the Pony Express — western Nevada. On a run in early May 1860, Haslam arrived at a station to find that all the horses were being used for an attack on the Paiutes. He watered and fed his tired horse, and they continued on.

Robert "Pony Bob" Haslam

a Pony Express station in St. Joseph, Missouri

He reached Buckland's station 75 miles (121 km) farther on. But the next rider was too afraid to go outside. So, Haslam changed horses and rode on. When he finally arrived at Smith Creek station, he had ridden 190 miles (306 km) straight. After a few hours' rest, he went all the way back to the station where he started. He rode 380 miles (611 km) in 36 hours — a Pony Express record.

The dedication of the Pony Express riders was remarkable. Riders delivered President Lincoln's **inaugural address** to California just seven days after it was made. In 18 months of Pony Express service, riders traveled 650,000 miles (1,046,071 km) sometimes under nearly impossible conditions. Through all that, only one rider was killed while on duty. Altogether about 200 riders worked for the Pony Express. Stations full of off-duty riders and station workers were in the most danger from Paiute attacks. The riders and station workers were true heroes of the American West.

inauguration of Abraham Lincoln at the unfinished Capitol building, March 4, 1861

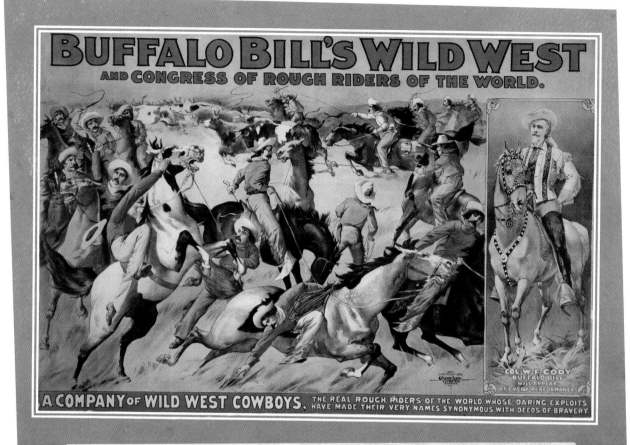

"Buffalo Bill" Cody

The most famous Pony Express rider might not have been a rider at all. Legend says William Cody, nicknamed Buffalo Bill, started his riding career at the age of 14. In reality, he worked briefly as a messenger for Russell, Majors, and Waddell at age 11.

Although he never technically worked for the Pony Express, Cody did much for its history. He grew up to be an expert storyteller and thrived on blending fact with fiction. One of his favorite topics was the Pony Express. He wrote about it in his autobiography and even included it in his hit show "Buffalo Bill's Wild West." His romanticized adventures captured audiences. His fame helped make the West and the Pony Express wildly popular pieces of history.

inaugural address—the speech a president gives when sworn into office

6

TELEGRAPH LINE EXPANSION

The telegraph was the first electronic device that communicated long-distance messages almost immediately. The device sent a series of dots and dashes, called Morse code, which could be translated into English. In 1844, a government-sponsored line connected Washington, D.C., to Baltimore, Maryland. From there, companies began to build lines throughout the United States.

On October 24, 1861, telegraph lines finally reached across the continent. Messages could be sent from one end of the country to the other instantly. The completion of this telegraph line sent the Pony Express out of business. However, even without the telegraph, the Pony Express would have had a hard time staying in business.

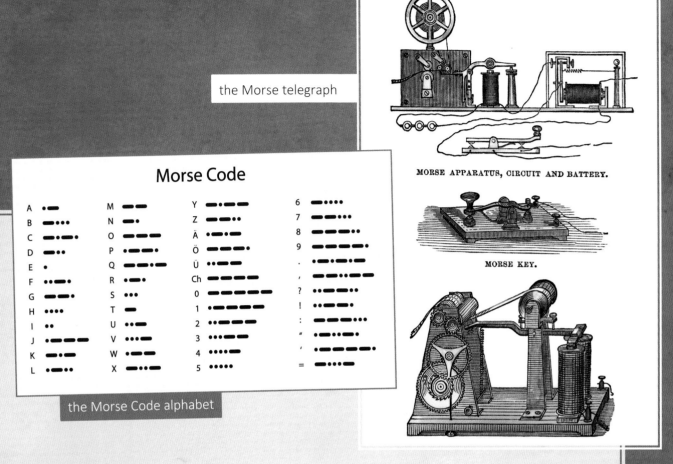

the Morse telegraph

Morse Code

A	·—	M	——	Y	—·——	6	—····
B	—···	N	—·	Z	——··	7	——···
C	—·—·	O	———	Ä	·—·—	8	———··
D	—··	P	·——·	Ö	———·	9	————·
E	·	Q	——·—	Ü	··——	.	·—·—·—
F	··—·	R	·—·	Ch	————	,	——··——
G	——·	S	···	0	—————	?	··——··
H	····	T	—	1	·————	!	—·—·——
I	··	U	··—	2	··———	:	———···
J	·———	V	···—	3	···——	"	·—··—·
K	—·—	W	·——	4	····—	'	·————·
L	·—··	X	—··—	5	·····	=	—···—

the Morse Code alphabet

Even though it was fast and efficient, the Pony Express did not make enough money. Russell, Majors, and Waddell spent $700,000 to get the Pony Express started and to keep it running. But in 18 months it only made $500,000, and the Paiute War in 1860 was costly. The Central Overland Company spent $75,000 to repair stations and replace horses during the conflict. After the Pony Express shut down, its owners suffered money problems.

The Pony Express helped maintain important contact with the West before and at the beginning of the Civil War. However, the government provided it with little support. By this time, the government was giving its money and attention to the Civil War.

Interest in the remarkable **feats** of the Pony Express was sparked again early in the 1900s. Pony Express riders began telling stories about their exciting adventures. Thanks to these stories, history remembers the riders crossing flooded streams, riding through blizzards, and trying to outride American Indian arrows.

DID YOU KNOW?
Western Union completed the transcontinental telegraph system on October 24, 1861, at Salt Lake City, Utah. Pony Express service halted two days later.

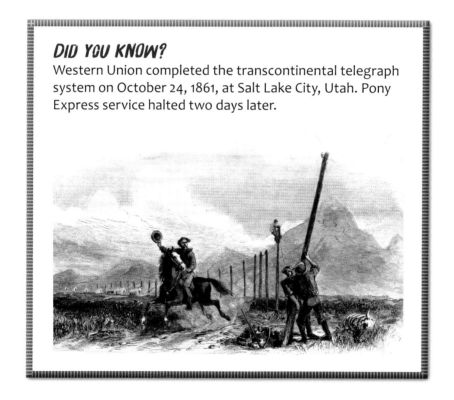

feat—outstanding achievement

movie poster of *Pony Express* (1953)

GLOSSARY

dedication (ded-uh-KAY-shuhn)—devotion; the act of giving your time, effort, or attention to some purpose

feat (FEET)—an outstanding achievement

freighting (FRAYT-ing)—transporting large amounts of goods

gateway (GATE-way)—a place where people can enter a region

inaugural address (in-AW-ger-ul ad-DRESS)—the speech a president gives when sworn into office

infrequent (in-FREE-kwuhnt)—not happening very often

oath (OHTH)—a serious, formal promise

political (puh-LIT-uh-kuhl)—of or relating to the government

postmaster general (POHST-mas-tur JEN-ur-uhl)—the head of the government's postal, or mail delivery, system

stagecoach (STAYJ-kohch)—a horse-drawn vehicle for carrying people and goods

telegraph (TEL-uh-graf)—a machine that uses electronic signals to send messages over long distances

terrain (tuh-RAYN)—the surface of the land

CRITICAL THINKING QUESTIONS

1. What were some of the challenges Pony Express riders faced on their routes?

2. What is one way the Pony Express could have stayed in business after the telegraph lines connected the country?

3. Why do you think stations were more vulnerable to attack than riders?

READ MORE

Micklos, John Jr. *A Primary Source History of the Gold Rush.* Primary Source History. North Mankato, Minn.: Capstone Press, 2016.

Micklos, John Jr. *Bold Riders: The Story of the Pony Express.* Adventures on the American Frontier. North Mankato, Minn.: Capstone Press, 2016.

Spies, Karen Borenmann. *Buffalo Bill Cody: Legend of the Wild West.* Legendary American Biographies. Berkeley Heights, N.J.: Enslow Publishing, 2015.

INTERNET SITES

Use Facthound to find Internet sites related to this book.

Visit *www.facthound.com*

Just type in 9781515771159 and go!

Check out projects, games and lots more at
www.capstonekids.com

INDEX